You Hold the Key to Finding Real Love

Sarah Reid

authorHOUSE

AuthorHouse™ UK
1663 Liberty Drive
Bloomington, IN 47403 USA
www.authorhouse.co.uk
Phone: 0800 047 8203 (Domestic TFN)
        +44 1908 723714 (International)

Published by AuthorHouse 07/26/2019

ISBN: 978-1-7283-8700-0 (sc)
ISBN: 978-1-7283-8699-7 (e)

Print information available on the last page.

Any people depicted in stock imagery provided by Getty Images are models, and such images are being used for illustrative purposes only.
Certain stock imagery © Getty Images.

This book is printed on acid-free paper.

Because of the dynamic nature of the Internet, any web addresses or links contained in this book may have changed since publication and may no longer be valid. The views expressed in this work are solely those of the author and do not necessarily reflect the views of the publisher, and the publisher hereby disclaims any responsibility for them.

Sarah Reid
www.book-me.co.uk

Contents

Introduction

Everybody wants and needs love; the real challenge is finding love that is genuine, healthy, and vibrant and that has no limits. In 2017 it was estimated that there were 16 million single people in the UK (http:// uk.parship.com). I remember a wise woman I once worked with who said, 'Love will either make you or break you.' I didn't understand what she meant, but now that I have matured, I totally understand the meaning of that phrase. I decided to write *You Hold the Key to Finding Real Love* because I feel too many of us grin and bear our relationships even if they are unhappy ones, because we think they will be going from the frying pan and into fire, or we may feel it is too much work. You are worthy of real love, and you deserve to be treated like a prince or princess, if only you will allow it.

I had to kiss quite a few frogs before I found my prince. I am not saying my relationship is perfect because no relationship is. The truth is it takes work, and you have to be prepared and willing to put in the work to reap your reward. I concentrated on the contents covered in this book because I believe the topics are the foundation to a well-functioning relationship. I am far from an expert at love, but I can say I have enough experience with relationships, which I think is valid. I would like to help others, even if it just a little bit, on their path to finding real love.

The idea of the book is that there are two questions for you to answer. This is the reason there is a blank space in the middle for you to write down your answers. Please take the time to reflect on your experiences before you write down your answers. You will be surprised at the way your answers spontaneously start to flow. My answers to the questions, which I have called 'My Scenario', are at the bottom of the page.

If you have struggled with finding your ideal partner, you may need to look deep within yourself, into areas that you are not aware of but that need to be addressed in order to avoid repeating the same mistakes. Why don't you take the love challenge and see what results you come up with? I dare you!

1

Communication

How would you describe good, effective communication?

Why and when do we need it in our relationships with others?

My Scenario

My husband and I have an informal chat at least once a week over dinner regarding all the positive things he noticed I did during the week. An example of how I made an impact on him includes suggestions on how we could improve our living space. In turn, I mention the positive things I noticed that he did to impact me. We discuss any issues that we did not appreciate and how we can move on from that. We decided to do this because we believe it keeps us on our toes and keeps our relationship healthy.

What would you say are your greatest communication challenges?

**How can a lack of communication become
a barrier within your relationship?**

My Scenario

I would say my greatest communication challenge was learning to talk through matters in the heat of an argument. I can be stubborn sometimes and often do not want to talk straightaway. My husband is the opposite and prefers to talk things through so we can resolve matters. Our plan now is to not go to bed while in an argument because the longer we leave it, the more tension there can be, which can widen the barrier and our resentment towards each other.

How important is listening in communication?

Is there a way we can measure or assess effective communication?

My Scenario

Listening is one of the most important factors in our relationship as we learn what we need from each other in order to flourish. Our way of measuring this is by reducing the arguments we may have.

**Can culture, gender, nationality, or social class
have an effect on communication?**

**Does it make it easier or harder to understand each other
when you're both from different backgrounds?**

My Scenario

With me coming from a Ghanaian heritage and my husband having a West Indian heritage, there were a few cultural differences that we came across. These included calling one's elders Uncle and Aunty on the Ghanaian side, whereas West Indians address most elders as Mr and Mrs as long as they were not one's real uncle or aunty. Sometimes when I say certain things to my husband, he thinks I am being authoritarian, but in fact I am simply saying this is what needs to be done. At first we could not understand this miscommunication, but we now realise it is a cultural difference in understanding how things are said and done.

What role do facial expressions, body language, gestures, and pauses play in communication?

Do you think nonverbal communication plays a big part in communication?

My Scenario

Nonverbal communication can include eye contact, body language, blinking, facial expressions, postures, and more. Nonverbal signals can increase trust and clarity and therefore can play a very important part in the information or message conveyed. They also include implicit messages (whether intentional or not), which are expressed through nonverbal behaviour. If one of us is a little annoyed with the other, we may prefer to say little verbally. We may answer the other with a shrug of the shoulders as a way of showing acknowledgement.

Has the development of the Internet and social media caused a change in the way we communicate?

My Scenario

Social media has indeed changed the way we communicate. Messages can travel around the world in a matter of seconds and can capture a very large audience when it comes to understanding someone or something in detail. It takes time to understand what someone is going through; this is where the intimate and personal interactions override social media. I personally prefer to sit down and talk about my day to a person face-to-face rather than read about how someone has spent his or her time.

Do you think we could benefit from communication courses?

My Scenario

I totally agree and believe that we have to take responsibility for what we say and what message reaches the other person. We have to take into account the communication styles of the people we are talking to. We should more carefully choose our words, facial expressions, gestures, and other body language. We need to make sure the messages we are trying to portray actually reach our counterparts. Factors such as gender, age, and culture have to be considered.

2

Honesty and Loyalty

How is trust important in our relationship?

What factors contribute to gaining trust?

My Scenario

Trusting each other plays a huge part in being honest with one another. I remember a time early in our relationship when I was a little under the weather and had to pay a contractor for work he had done in my home. The problem was going to the cash machine to get the cash. I had to ask my partner to run this errand for me. I was a little nervous giving him my card and PIN because I had never done this before. But at the same time, I did trust him. Later that evening, I checked my account online and was assured that the right amount was taken out and my balance was right. He passed the test, which meant a great deal to me.

What are the benefits of working together as a team?

Does it make it easier or complicate things?

My Scenario

Two heads working together are surely better than one. In relationships, you often have to compromise and understand one another's needs and wants. Work out together how you are going to make it happen. In our relationship, we both work so we are both tired by the time we get home. We find the way that works for us is cooking dinner together. This gives us a chance to talk about our day, and it really does take the burden off one person who may have to cook for the family. Before we realise it we are sitting down at the table and eating dinner!

**Are you tolerant or intolerant in accepting
your partner's imperfections?**

How important is acceptance to you?

My Scenario

There is no such thing as a perfect relationship. Imperfection is real and is a beautiful thing because it shows how two people accept one another and deal with the imperfections to make it ideal. In the beginning of our relationship, I quickly noticed the similarities we had, but once we began living together, I soon found out some habits he had that did not go down too well, such as leaving up the toilet lid. I remember feeling not so good after I would moan to him about why he constantly forgot to put it down. To keep the peace, when he did forget to put it down, I would simply lower it. I have learnt that your happiness grows in direct proportion to your partner's acceptance—and in inverse proportion to your partner's intolerance and expectations.

Do you believe that forgiveness can help to set you free?

How did you feel when you forgave someone?

My Scenario

It is a fact that unforgiveness can cause destruction, strife, and confusion, whether consciously or unconsciously. It can cause bitterness in your relationships, and it can feel like a heavy burden on your shoulders. Why carry this around when you can be set free? As a child, I remember certain things that happened between my parents that were unsettling for me. This left me with trust issues in my relationships as an adult. I did not understand at first why I found it so hard to trust men, but after analysing and reflecting, I now understand that it is what I internalised as a child. I truly believed that all men were the same. As I mentioned earlier, I would have a mental checklist for the men who came into my life, and if they passed, then I would get to know them. I decided to forgive my father for the things I had witnessed as a child, which made me feel much better and found my relationships were much healthier thereafter.

Would you say that you are empathetic in your relationships?

Are there expectations when you show empathy to someone?

My Scenario

I would say I naturally have the ability to sense other people's emotions and imagine what someone else might be thinking or feeling. If I can help someone in any way, then I will. I have been told many times that I have excellent interpersonal skills and would make a good counsellor. Sometimes this can be taken for granted, and my kind nature can be seen as a form of weakness and taken advantage of. Unfortunately, I have experienced this quite a few times with people I thought were my friends. I was there for them, but when I needed support, I did not receive it in return. It was a hard time but was a big wake-up call because I really did find out who were my friends and who were not. This in turn made it easier for me to let go of some friendships.

How much would you say you love yourself?

Note to Self

Relationships do not create happiness; they simply reflect it. Happiness and joy come from deep down within. If you are broken, there is a chance that your relationships will not be healthy, especially if your partner is also broken. Relationships are simply mirrors of the combined joy that two people have as individuals.

Never feel guilty about removing toxic people from your life because they are a hindrance rather than a blessing. You are beautiful, unique, and powerful when you love yourself, so stand in the mirror and tell yourself this.

3

Understanding

How well do you think you know your partner?

**How long did you spend getting to know your
partner before you became exclusive?**

My Scenario

It is important to learn how to understand others if you don't know their strengths, their joys, their fears, and their imperfections. In my past relationships, I did not always take the time to get to know them before committing myself to a relationship. As a result, the relationships never seemed to work out. My husband and I were friends for at least nine months; within this period, we courted each other without going to one another's houses, and we got to know one another before we agreed to become exclusive. We both believe the dating period is a crucial time to become comfortable with one another, especially if one wants the relationship to last. We have faith that our marriage will last forever.

Are you aware of your own feelings and motivations?

How much would you say you understand your partner?

My Scenario

It is hard to understand another person if you do not even understand yourself! I can truly put my hand on my heart and say I know when my husband is happy or sad, or if there is something bothering him by his demeanour. I remember he came home from work one day, and although he was talking the same as usual, I could sense that something was wrong. I asked him a few times if everything was fine, and he said it was, but he later confessed to me that evening that he was unhappy at work and was thinking of leaving. You should always trust your instincts because they are normally right.

Do you impose your beliefs on your partner?

What happens when your ideals are forced upon your partner?

My Scenario

In our relationship, we respect each other's opinions and views. When we do not agree on something, we leave it at that and agree to disagree. I am not going to lie: sometimes it is frustrating when I just want him to agree with me on something. But that would be selfish of me. It is not right to think that you are better than anyone else or that what you think is right. Doing so will leave you unaware of how your partner really feels. If you want to be understanding you should respect your partner's convictions. Accept others' beliefs as part of who they are. Hopefully doing this will keep your bond stronger.

**How often do you and your partner have time
apart to spend with family and friends?**

Would you say your relationship has a healthy balance?

My Scenario

One of my previous relationships was unhealthy. Marcus wanted us to always be together day and night. He tried to control who and when I could see my family and friends. At first I found it flattering that Marcus always wanted to be with me, and I thought it was real love. The element of control that Marcus had over me was unbelievable, and I knew I had to get out of that relationship.

In my marriage, although we spend a great deal of quality time together, we both take time at least once a week to be apart with our family and friends.

Are you quick to react to something your partner did?

**Do you tend to want to resolve a problem immediately
or when things have calmed down?**

My Scenario

I have to admit that I used to be fast at reacting to something without giving my husband a chance to explain himself. What made matters worse was that he always remained calm, which used to wind me up. I often found when I calmed down and gave him the chance to explain himself, I could see where I had jumped to a conclusion. Sometimes angry outbursts can lead to something being said that you did not mean to say, and it can be damaging to the other person especially, if he or she is sensitive. I can happily say I have learnt to not be so quick to be judgemental. You can resolve matters a lot faster when you remain calm and talk about the problem.

Do you help your partner learn from his or her mistakes?

Do you prefer to keep mistakes that you have made to yourself?

My Scenario

Being understanding is one of the best ways to fix a problem in a relationship. It can help you to heal and understand that if your partner has made a mistake, he or she deserves a second chance to prove himself or herself. Someone I know had trust issues with men because she had been cheated on quite a few times. The partner she is currently with is a bit of a workaholic, but she was convinced he was cheating on her, so she contacted a private investigator via email and forgot to clear the history of searches on her computer. Long story short, he found out about it and was so furious that he wanted to end their relationship because he was fed up with all the accusations made against him and the distrust. After pleading with him and asking for forgiveness, he agreed to give her one more chance. They are currently both going to counselling sessions, which seems to be helping, and their relationship is going from strength to strength.

Encourage your partner to be open with you.

It is best that you are both open with each other, especially about things that can directly or indirectly affect your relationship. Some people may find it hard to express in words their thoughts and innermost feelings, so it takes patience to understand where they are coming from. If you think your relationship is a good one, then it is worthwhile investing time into making it work.

4

Patience

**Would you say you have the patience to make
the most of your relationship?**

What attributes would you say it takes to show patience?

My Scenario

We tend to be less patient with those who are closest to us. When we act impatiently towards someone, it can be very hurtful, and it can seem like we do not value or care about that person. Sometimes my husband has a habit of beating around the bush when he is explaining something before he gets to the point. Although I love him with all my heart, I can sometimes get a bit impatient and ask him to get to the point. He thinks I am being insulting, but I really do not mean it like that. I am simply eager to find out what happened. It took someone doing the same thing to me for me to know how my husband felt, and it was not a nice feeling. I now take it upon myself to be a bit more patient. I will get to hear the story even if it takes time.

Does your relationship need nurturing?

Do you feel like the stress of the day can zap your patience?

My Scenario

I think it is impossible to learn to love all of your partner's ways in spite of his or her faults. It takes work to learn to accept others for who they are and to compromise with each other when problems arise. Good relationships do not just happen; they are tended to and nurtured. There is so much pressure on us in this busy world, but it is still important to nurture our relationships; doing so eliminates one less stress in our lives. We carry this out in our relationship by having a date night at least once every fortnight. We spend this time talking to each other. I want to point out that it is equally important to feel comfortable around your partner in silence; it brings out an intimate closeness towards each other that really strengthens the bond.

Patience is love.
Love is patient.

They say patience is a virtue. Nowadays too many people walk away from the challenges of developing patience in love relationships. In fact, it is a great opportunity for personal growth. When you look inwards together, you may be astounded at want you discover.

You either allow impatience to get the best of you, making you miserable and ruining any chance of a healthy relationship, or you get over it.

5

The Five Love Languages

What are the five love languages?

**Does it seem like you and your spouse are
speaking two different languages?**

My Scenario

By identifying, understanding, and speaking your partner's love language, you may find that your relationship manoeuvres more smoothly.

>Words of affirmation: Words that build up another person. 'You look beautiful in your dress. It really compliments your figure.'

>Gifts: They show that you were thinking about the person.

>Acts of service: Do something for your spouse that you know he or she would appreciate, like washing dishes, doing the shopping, or cleaning the house.

>Quality time: Give your partner your undivided attention. Talk and listen to one another, or take a walk together.

>Physical touch: Show expressions of love such as holding hands, hugging, kissing, and making love.

How do you know your love language?

What does your love language mean?

My Scenario

My husband and I were both born in the same month, November. We share the same star sign, which makes us quite similar: we're sensitive, affectionate, and loving. My love languages are words of affirmation and quality time. My husband's love languages are words of affirmation and physical touch. People whose love language is words of affirmation tend to be natural and forthcoming with their words. We both enjoy exchanging many texts messages when we are apart, and we sometimes send cards with meaningful words and messages to one another. It has really helped that my husband and I share at least one love language because the words we say to one another affirms our love and tells us how much we care. We are inattentive to our needs, we take time and make sure we fulfill our other love languages which are quality time and physical touch, so our needs are not lacking in these areas of importance.

Why you should know your partner's love language?

In relationships, people's style of thinking could be different from what their needs are. It is therefore crucial that you understand what your partner's love language of love is so you unintentionally avoid hurting one another's feelings. Believe me, it will make your life much easier if you learn your partner's love language. Are you aware of what your and your partner's love languages are?

Relationship Prompts

1. You and your partner have been together for a few years when they forget your birthday. You wait all day for them to acknowledge it, but by the next morning, they still haven't said a word. What would you do?
2. You and your partner have not really been intimate lately, so you sit down to talk about it. They say that they want to experiment and ask if you'd be willing to open the relationship for a trial period. What would you do?
3. On your wedding day, you find out that your partner has been having an affair. You confront them about it, and they swear that it's over. The wedding is all paid for, and your guests have started to arrive. Would you end the relationship?
4. You've been with your partner for a little while when you find out they cheated in their last relationship. It was not that they were unhappy or that there were problems in the relationship; they simply slipped up. What would you do?
5. You find out from somebody else that your partner has kissed another person. You thought you were both happy, and there seems to be no reason for it. What would you do?
6. Your partner tells you that they had sexual relations with somebody else. Their excuse is that they were extremely drunk, and they seem sincerely sorry about it. Would you end the relationship?
7. You find out your partner has been messaging somebody else. The messages are flirty, and you are not happy with them, but as far as you're aware, your partner hasn't met up with the person they're texting. What would you do?
8. Your partner is a very flirty person, and you know it's their personality. You have no reason to think they're cheating on you, but their flirting makes you feel uncomfortable. What would you do?
9. Your bedroom action is literally non-existent! You and your partner just don't seem compatible in bed at all, no matter how many times you've tried. Would you end the relationship?

10. After dating for a couple of weeks, you make plans for your partner to meet your best friend. Later, your friend pulls you to one side and explains that they don't like your partner at all. What would you do?

11. Your partner talks about their ex a fair bit. They've assured you they're 100 per cent over the relationship and would never get back with the ex, but the topic keeps coming up. What would you do?

12. You and your partner sit down to have a serious conversation about where your relationship is going, and you learn they do not want to ever get married. Would you end the relationship?

13. Your partner seems to make fun of you in front of people in an attempt to make everybody else laugh. You don't really think much of it to begin with, but it soon becomes a regular occurrence, and it irritates you. What would you do?

14. Your partner has no drive and ambition. They have a job but are satisfied with remaining at the same level. They have no desire to move towards a promotion or better themselves, and they seem to be very lazy. What would you do?

15. Your partner always seems to cancel each time you arrange to go out. What would you do?

Afterword

I believe that we all have a soulmate out there. Once you find him or her, you must work together to lay a solid foundation.

Applying what you have learnt about yourself in this book should improve your relationship. Everything in life is a working progress. It depends on whether you are prepared to put in the work. If you are, you shall surely reap the rewards at the end.

www.ingramcontent.com/pod-product-compliance
Lightning Source LLC
Chambersburg PA
CBHW051414250726
48655CB00003B/1040